In Person
THE PRINCE AND
PRINCESS OF WALES

A L A S T A I R   B U R N E T
Photographs by Tim Graham

This book is produced with the co-operation of
Their Royal Highnesses The Prince and Princess of Wales

INDEPENDENT TELEVISION NEWS LIMITED
in association with
MICHAEL O'MARA BOOKS LIMITED

First published in Great Britain by Independent Television News Limited
in association with Michael O'Mara Books Limited,
20 Queen Anne Street, London W1N 9FB, 1985

ISBN 0 948397 25 X

Designed by Martin Bristow
Editors: Jane Heller and Georgina Evans
Picture research by Tomás Graves

Video film processed by BPCC Video Graphics
Typeset by SX Composing Limited
Printed and bound by Printer Industria Gráfica SA,
Barcelona, Spain
D.L.B. 37218-1985

ACKNOWLEDGMENTS

The following photographs by Tim Graham are the copyright of
The Trustees of the Prince of Wales' Charities Trust:
jacket photographs; 1, 2, 13-13, 14-15, 21 (below), 33, 35, 36-37,
38-39, 40, 48 (top right and below), 53, 87, 98 (below), 99, 100,
104-113, 120, 121 (below), 122-123, 124-125

Video stills by ITN are the copyright of The Trustees of the
Prince of Wales' Charities Trust: 18-19, 34, 42-43

Additional photographs are reproduced by kind permission of the following:
By gracious permission of Her Majesty the Queen: 55
Associated Newspapers: 114 (below)
Camera Press: 26 (Lichfield), 64 both (Colin Davey), 114 above (David Beal)
Syndication International: 80, 85
Topham: 61, 62-63

All other photographs are copyright © Tim Graham

CONTENTS

THE PARTNERS

Theirs is a partnership, and it works. They are busy, very much in love, and trying to do their job, pleasing people, working for people, day by day. But they are still working out, day by day, just what their job is, and just what people expect it to be.

The Prince of Wales, with thirty-seven years' experience, is cautious about it all: 'It is, more than anything else, a way of life. It's more than just a job. It's a complete, 24-hour-a-day business, really.'

The Princess, just four years into the mission, is modest: "I feel my role is supporting my husband whenever I can, and always being behind him, encouraging him. And also, most important, being a mother and a wife. And that's what I try to achieve. Whether I do is another thing, but I do try.'

It's never been an easy job. The Black Prince managed it in the fourteenth century by helping to thrash the French at Crécy and actually capturing the French King at Poitiers. But, since him, there have not been all that many successes as Prince of Wales. Indeed, apart from Princess (and later Queen) Alexandra a century ago, there have not been many popular Princesses of Wales.

Prince Charles spells it out: 'The sovereign obviously has a set role to perform within the constitution, but the heir to the throne doesn't. And you could

The Prince and Princess of Wales have a unique task to fulfil in the modern world. 'They are busy, very much in love and trying to do their job.' (Previous spread) At Maitland in Australia in August 1983 and returning from the Garter Day Service at St George's Chapel, Windsor, in June 1985

Ambassadors at home and abroad – the Prince and Princess during their tour of Italy in April 1985 after a private audience with Pope John Paul II at the Vatican

easily sit around and do nothing.'

(That is, of course, precisely what his great-uncle, who ended up Duke of Windsor, thought – and often did.)

He turns to her: 'People expect a great deal of us, I think, and I'm always conscious – I'm sure you are, too, darling – of not wanting to let people down, not wanting to let this country down.'

So they are, in their own minds, internal ambassadors in a real sense, as well as being regular ambassadors abroad in the United States, Australia, Canada, Italy. He has a list of good causes to support that far outnumber the regiments whose uniform he

wears; collectors of City director-ships have simple, undemanding lives compared with his. So far the Princess has one regiment, the Royal Hampshires; one RAF station, Wittering; and one county cricket eleven, Glou-cestershire (it's been one of their better seasons). But she's been selective: 'I don't want to dive into something without being able to follow it up. Nothing would upset me more than just being a name on top of a piece of paper and not showing any in-terest at all.'

She has become increasingly concerned about young people hooked on drugs: 'I felt that,

In the spring of 1981 Prince Charles visited President Reagan at the White House (right), while in Australia in 1983 (below) the Prince and Princess of Wales met Prime Minister Bob Hawke and his wife in Canberra

The Princess's first RAF station. In June 1985 the Princess of Wales accepted the position of Honorary Air Commodore of RAF Wittering, a Harrier base near Peterborough. During her visit to the station on 25 September the Princess reviewed a guard of honour consisting of one hundred personnel – a duty she had not previously undertaken. She was then taken on a tour of the base and inspected aircraft and armaments

being twenty-four – and a lot of the people who are on drugs are possibly around that age – I felt I could start off by showing some interest, and not just going to an engagement and then walking away.'

She is especially impressed by the work of the hospices for the terminally ill: 'After I had been round the first ward, I remember it so vividly, I was struck by the calmness of the patients in their beds, confronting their illness. They were so brave about it and made me feel so humble.'

And she admires Dr Barnardo's homes, particularly their work with mentally-handicapped children. How did that interest start?

'You see, I've got very healthy strong boys, and it's not always the case with the families I'm meeting through Dr Barnardo's. I realise how incredibly lucky I am, and I don't know how I could cope if I had a child who was handicapped or mentally handi-capped in some way.

'So I'm going out there to meet these children, and I'm learning all the time and trying to understand, trying desperately to understand how they cope.'

To them both, their own young sons are an unending source of delight and pleasure. Prince William roams the house at Kensington Palace, with a word for every visitor. It may be just as well for his future that he is

The Princess of Wales is developing her own personal interests; many of them associated with children and the elderly. She is President of Dr Barnardo's and on 10 October 1985 she visited mentally handicapped children and their families at the Home in Salford, Greater Manchester (above)

On the same day she found time also to visit St Anne's Hospice, Heald Green in Manchester (near right). The Princess greatly admires the work of such hospices and their 'welcoming, homely atmosphere'. On 11 October, in the East End of London, she visited St Joseph's Hospice, Hackney, bringing much joy to the people she met (opposite)

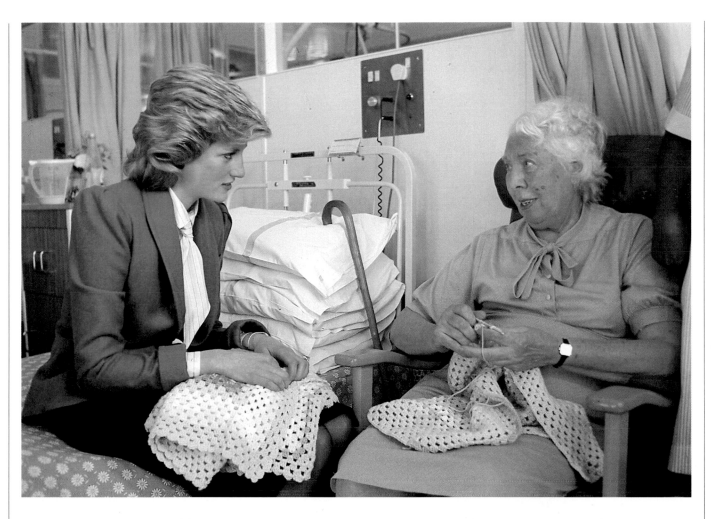

not, and has never been, put off by television cameras. And Prince Harry is, in his own determined way, highly mobile about the place too.

Was the Princess a little sad when Prince William went off to nursery school?

'Well, I was because it's opening another chapter in my life, and certainly William's. But he's ready for it. He's a very independent child. He's surrounded by a tremendous amount of grown-ups, so his conversation's very forthright.'

So what did he really think of his first day at school?

'He was just so excited by it all, and there was a tremendous spurt of conversation. If you could understand that, you could understand anything; he was trying to get it all out.

'But he just adores other children, and he's very much an organiser – which probably might be helpful in future years. He really loved it.'

In fact, Prince William is so clued-up about most things that starting at school was apparently a show he not only starred in, he ran it himself: 'Oh yes, he was so organised that day that he chose his shorts and shirt, and it's best to let him do that if you want him to smile at the cameras.'

Will he be organising his own press releases quite soon? 'He might. He's got a mother that might be a bit worried about that.'

'The young princes are an unending source of delight and pleasure' to their parents

'Prince William is very enthusiastic about things and pushes himself into it . . . Henry is quieter.' Prince William is not at all shy in front of the cameras (above) and, undeterred (below), helps his mother prepare for more photographs before he joins Prince Henry at the piano

The parents are enjoying the experience of both boys doing new things each day. And there are differences that a mother's eye can spot: 'William's a typical three-year-old – because I worked with three-year-olds. Very enthusiastic about things, pushes himself right into it. He's not at all shy, but very polite, extraordinarily enough. Where, perhaps, Harry is quieter and just watches. Whether he copies William we'll wait and see, but he's certainly a different character altogether.'

But not entirely different. The two of them hammering at the piano produces a discordance with which they are jointly very happy. 'Sounds like Stockhausen,' their father says. The Princess still plays the piano herself: 'I fiddle around: it's nothing to get excited about, but it's marvellous, it's very therapeutic.' Her sons plainly find it a therapy, or something, too.

This is the private world they like so much, the family world that matters.

The outside world expects to see a royal example in a normally happy family life. It also expects to see the royal partnership on view, as it did with King George

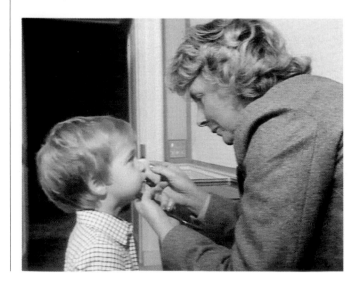

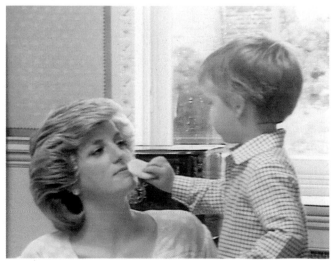

VI and Queen Elizabeth, and does now with the Queen and the Duke of Edinburgh.

But family life is not always what the partnership of the Prince and Princess can organise for itself. The calls on them do not always call for both of them; and in the modern world they see some advantages in that.

How do they set about it? The Prince is candid. It's not exactly co-ordinated in advance:

'Well, rather probably more haphazardly than people would think. We tend to have two programme meetings a year, which means that you have to plan your life six months or more ahead, which is murder.

'But, I mean, you decide if you want to come on a particular thing with me . . .

'There will obviously be occasions when, you know, we do things separately, and I think that's a good thing. I don't think one should do everything together all the time.'

So does the Princess put her foot down and say what she wants to go to, and what not? Not quite. It seems there's protocol to be observed:

'That's a naughty question. No, if I'm asked, if the invitation

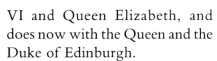

comes in, would they both like to come, obviously I'll try. But sometimes I'm not required. If it's sort of what I call a boys' day, and they don't want me, I'll go somewhere else.'

It is a little hard to believe that the Princess isn't included in every invitation, but that seems to be how part of British society, even in this day and age, still goes about its social life. They both say it makes it difficult to meet their friends as often as they'd both like. That's especially true on weekdays. The Princess says:

'I sometimes have my friends to lunch if my husband's out. We have people to dinner whenever we can, but my husband goes to a lot of dinners where wives aren't required, so we can't always find a date to suit both of us.'

When Walter Bagehot, the Victorian constitutionalist, ob-served that a royal family was 'an interesting idea', even though in his day it chiefly comprised 'a re-tired widow and an unemployed youth', and much of its reporting for the avid middle class was con-fined to the staid phraseology of the Court Circular, he had no conception of what an under-statement that was. If royalty has adapted better to the last quarter of the twentieth century than most British institutions, grasp-ing the essential point that vir-tually all medieval ceremony must have been designed with television in mind, it is no less true that the price of its adapta-tion has been paid, and is still paid every day, by the royal family itself.

In the past two years there have been no fewer than 112 books published about the Princess alone, selling, it is thought, 27

There are occasions when the Prince and Princess do things separately. In August 1984 Prince Charles visited Papua New Guinea (opposite) to open the new Parliament building and was made 'supreme chief' on the island of Manus. While soon after Prince Henry's birth the Princess visited a Family Centre in Ealing (right) – run by the National Deaf-Blind and Rubella Association, another of her interests. On 14 October 1985 Prince Charles met Mr Rajiv Gandhi, Prime Minister of India, at Kensington Palace

million copies in Britain and abroad. The newspaper stories cannot be counted. They and the magazine covers, which sell because she is on them, give publishers profits, and journalists and printers work. Then there are the professional imitators, some of whom are better than others: flattery, in a way, but a form of flattery which previous royal generations did not have to live with. Hairdressers and valets tell tales. And the cartoonists; to them the royal family is like anyone else nowadays, only more so. Most of it is meant well, although there are doubts at Kensington Palace if something like the 'Spitting Image' productions really are well meant. But there is no escape.

The royal strength is continuity. British history, like English and Scottish law, is measured by the dates of its sovereigns. Plain people identify events by royal occasions, not by the haphazard dates of general elections. That means that royal families, even royal children, are always on parade, even when they are supposed to be enjoying themselves. One frown, one slip, one word and it's a headline.

Children are less rare in the White House than they are in No. 10 Downing Street, but, although all politicians' children attract attention and interest while their parents are winning elections, they are forgotten almost as soon as the parental furniture is moved out. The Wilson boys, even the Thatcher twins, all have unobserved and unspectacular lives ahead of them, if they wish. It is not at all so with the Prince and Princess of Wales and their family.

They are the first Prince and Princess of Wales to live their lives in the vortex of the modern media. Whatever the cartoonists made of the Prince Regent, or the radical newspapers of Edward VII's exploits when he was Prince of Wales, there has never before been the relentless inquisitiveness of television, newspapers and radio of the kind there is today. Gossipers, fantasists, even astrologers all feel they have to contribute.

They both have something to say about that.

On 15 November 1984 the Princess launched Royal Princess, *P&O's new de luxe liner*

ON THE RECORD

If part of the job is to get the image right – and it is – how are they to go about it? They have to start with the wedding, when they first stepped before the world together, and the recollection of which is at the back of at least 700 million people's memories whenever they see them going about their job now. What are their own memories? The Princess vividly recalls the anxieties she didn't show then: 'It was terrifying. It was such a long walk up that aisle for a start. No, I'm only teasing ... Am I?'

The Prince says he enjoyed it enormously. That was partly because he had looked forward to organising it, arranging the music, and having it in St Paul's, where he was 'terribly keen to have it'.

'I found we were carried along on a wave of enormous friendliness and enthusiasm. It was remarkable. And I kept telling myself anyway to remember this for as long as I could, because it was such a unique experience.'

They own up, a little ruefully, to the responses that neither of them got precisely right. The Princess is sure she married the right man, even though she got his names wrong: 'Well, with four names it's quite something to get organised.'

And it turns out he did, in fact, endow her with all his worldly goods, even if it didn't quite come out like that. It was nervousness? 'Yes, but it added a certain amount of amusement into the proceedings.'

Their memories, the serious memories, are optimistic. The Princess says she thinks of 'just everybody getting on with everybody. Everybody happy, smiling, all problems out of the way, and people could look forward to something. That's what I think is so terribly important, to

The Prince and Princess of Wales faced the world together on the day of their wedding, 29 July 1981 (previous spread). The Princess recollects, 'It was such a long walk up that aisle', while Prince Charles thinks 'It would be great fun to do it again.' It was a wonderfully happy day not only for the bride and groom and their attendants (above) but also for their family and friends, and above all for the millions of spectators around the world

look forward, because a lot of people have difficult lives, difficult problems, and to have something to look forward to is so essential.'

The Prince: 'It would be great fun to do it again.'

The Princess: 'My father says that the whole time.'

And the Prince remembers looking out from his own room at Buckingham Palace to the Victoria Memorial at the top of the Mall on the night before the wedding:

'All night people were sitting out on the steps there singing "Rule Britannia" and every kind of thing. It really was remarkable, and I found myself standing in the window with tears pouring down my face.

'Inevitably these things don't always last very long, but I think it made one realise that underneath everything else, all the rowing and the bickering and disagreements that go on the rest of the time, every now and then you get a reason for a celebration or a feeling of being a nation.'

Something of that comes back on royal tours, when there is a sense of occasion, of rarity, and they themselves feel they are engaged in doing something specifically for the country. They both say one of the things they can do is achieve what the Prince calls 'a positive atmosphere towards Britain'.

'I would also like to hope that maybe through trying to engender that sort of awareness and

interest in Britain, that other things would follow, like increased trade and export opportunities.

'This is an area which, I feel, hasn't really been concentrated on enough in fact, in following up as quickly as possible what openings we might have been able to make. It's very difficult for us to say how much can be achieved, but I think it is important that good will is created. And it's amazing, sometimes, what can be achieved through good will.'

This is where to many people, especially tour organisers, the Princess's clothes are of the first importance in generating extra admiration and interest. They're what all good tour reporters try to have a column or two about for people back home. But she is not quite as enthusiastic. How much time does she have to give to them?

'Not as much as, perhaps, people think. My clothes are not my priority. I enjoy bright colours and my husband likes to see me look smart, presentable, but fashion isn't my big thing at all.

'Obviously, if I'm helping the fashion industry and helping the British side of things, well, that's marvellous, but I never tried to do that, and I do think there's too much emphasis on my clothes.'

That can be a little difficult to believe, as any fashion she adopts turns into a fad among the brighter young things.

The Princess does not consider her clothes a priority. She does, however, enjoy bright colours and sometimes likes to be a little outrageous. In April 1985 in Venice (left) the Princess wore a dazzling green coat-dress and hat, while in Florence (right) she chose a flamboyant black and blue dress by one of her newer designers

'When I first arrived there were a lot of people to help me.' At the start of her honeymoon cruise in Gibraltar the Princess wore a romantic crêpe-de-chine dress and jacket by Donald Campbell and for the end of the cruise she chose a gorgeous peach crêpe georgette outfit by Benny Ong. The couple's time at Balmoral demanded warmer clothes and for the photocall by the Brig o'Dee the Princess wore a hounds-tooth check suit by Bill Pashley

But doesn't going away on tour really mean quite a bit of work for her?

'Well, it was when we first went on tour after we got married. I had to buy endless new things, of course, because on a tour you change three or four times a day, and I had to buy new things.

'That was the problem. The arrival of all the new things was causing tremendous criticism, but what else could I do? I couldn't go around in a leopard skin.'

Does she take her husband's advice about what to wear? Apparently, not very often:

The Princess: 'I ask him if this looks right or that looks right, but the chances of turning up in what he says are absolutely nil.'

The Prince: 'She asks me, you see, "Which one do I wear?" I say, "Well, why don't you wear that one?" '

The Princess: 'I go in the other one.'

The Prince: 'She turns up in something else. Why do you ask me?'

The Princess: 'I don't know.'

The Prince: 'But I do. You know, I like seeing a lady well dressed. It was one of the things I always noticed about her before we got married. She had, I thought, a very good sense of style and design.'

So how does the Princess pick her designers? Are they recommended to her?

'When I first arrived there were a lot of people to help me. It's now really my own choice, but I can't always wear what I'd like to an engagement because it's just not practical.

'You'd be amazed what one has to worry about, from the obvious things like the wind – because there's always a gale wherever we go – and the wind is my enemy, there's no doubt about that.

'And you've got to put your

One of the things Prince Charles noticed about the Princess before they were married was her 'good sense of style and design'. She has always loved warm sweaters with colourful patterns (opposite) and this jersey was an early acquisition. Her stylishness and elegance are clearly evident in her more formal outfits such as the red and blue silk crêpe-de-chine two-piece (right) first worn at Nicholas Soames' wedding in May 1981

Everything will be seen 'time and time again because . . . it still works'. The Princess cleverly adapts her outfits for different occasions. The double-breasted pink suit (opposite) worn with a tie-neck blouse has also been teamed with other high-collared blouses. When planning her wardrobe for visits and tours such as those in Canada and Italy, the Princess adds, 'There are so many things to worry about . . . the wind is my enemy . . . and you can't have hems too short . . . Clothes are for the job.' But despite all these considerations the Princess remains the essence of style. Seen (opposite) at Hammersmith Hospital, Edmonton in Canada, Sicily, Ottawa in Canada, and (below) visiting Cardigan in Wales on 9 October 1985

arm up to get some flowers, so you can't have something too revealing, and you can't have hems too short because when you bend over there's six children looking up your skirt.' There is only one golden rule: 'Clothes are for the job. They've got to be practical. Sometimes I can be a little outrageous, which is quite nice. Sometimes.'

So that after getting off planes 'with a sort of Force 10 gale blowing me on one side' and having 'to anchor my hats on practically with nails', it was really a relief to visit an oil rig out in the North Sea – wearing the proper oil rig outfit: 'Well, that was wonderful. To me they were very special people. It wasn't an outfit, it was just practical.

Otherwise, you know, had we ended up in the sea, we would have had problems.'

And what does she think of the critics who say they've seen such and such a dress before? Some of the Italians were a little disappointed, they said, when that happened there:

'Well, I'm afraid you're going to see everything time and time again because it fits, it's comfortable, and it still works. You know, I feel that a lot of people thought I was going on a fashion tour for two weeks. I wasn't. I was going along to support the British flag, with my husband, as his wife. My clothes were far from my mind.'

She has come a long way, as they have come a long way to-

The Prince and Princess 'have come a long way together' since their wedding day. Today they both enjoy their family life immensely – and 'the partnership is thriving' (opposite, below and following pages)

gether, in the four years since the wedding on 29 July 1981. He seems, in a real sense, a happier, more fulfilled, man, enjoying with his own young family the home life he enjoyed so much as a boy. No one was surprised at the story that he got Prince William used to having baths by climbing into the bath with him.

She, in turn, has learned a lot. She is visibly acquiring new confidence now with every public engagement she has. It is no longer the 'shy Di' that people,

without actually realising it, were apt to patronise. Now she is happy to sound off about television programmes that she thinks unsuitable for her sons, and to pick a horse for a pensioner who likes his daily bet. (It lost, but he didn't care.)

If she ever had any doubts, she has come through them. If there is any unfriendliness in store anywhere, she seems equipped to see it off. She has never lacked courage anyway. The partnership is thriving.

FACING THE WORLD

Their wedding at St Paul's on 29 July 1981 went off so well in the eyes of the world that it has been an almost impossible act to follow. But the Prince and Princess are triers, and they have been sensible. The romantic image has been turned almost unerringly into the young family image.

Most of the world has been delighted by it. He says she keeps him young. She is slimmer, more stunningly beautiful than she was. He has lost much of the naval manner: the public perception is no longer of a prince in uniform. He has long since stopped parachuting and diving under the Arctic ice and steeplechasing – the tests he set himself to prove himself.

Now it is his artistic side that is coming out, and marriage is helping to bring out: music, the arts (he enjoyed that side of their visit to Italy especially), even a little sketching of his own. She, in turn, has taken up the causes that interest her and that she can help.

But this is the first international royal family, faced every day with the curiosity of the international media. Many of those who write about them know what they're writing about. Much of the television and radio coverage is appreciated. But, without going quite as far as the Sunday papers in France, there are stories printed that don't exactly ring true at Kensington Palace. So what does the Princess say when she reads that she's a determined, domineering woman?

The Princess is 'slimmer, more stunningly beautiful than she was'. Looking slim and elegant (previous spread) she was photographed at Kensington Palace in October 1985 while she looked stunningly beautiful attending the première of the film 'Octopussy' on 6 June 1983

The Prince 'seems . . . a happier, more fulfilled man, enjoying with his own young family the home life he enjoyed so much as a boy' (above and below)

'I don't always read that. I'm – people are very willing to tell me that, but I don't think I am. I'm a perfectionist with myself, but not necessarily with everyone else. Those stories arose a long time ago, and have kept coming out again and again. But I don't think I am.'

Is she hurt by these stories?

'Well, obviously, you feel very wounded. You think: oh gosh, I don't want to go out and do my engagement this morning, nobody wants to see me, help, panic.

'But you've got to push yourself out and remember that some people, hopefully, won't believe everything they read about you.

'There is far too much about me in the newspapers, far too much. It horrifies me, when there's more important things, like what goes on in the hospices, or there's been a bomb or something.'

Does she, then, have any sense of living in rivalry with Princess Anne, as is said time and time again?

'None at all. Princess Anne's been working incredibly hard for the Save the Children Fund, and I'm her biggest fan because what she crams into a day I could never

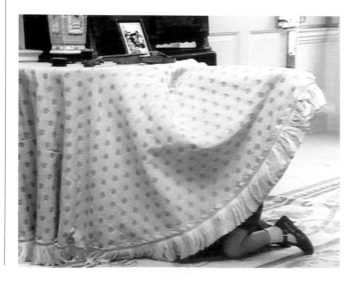

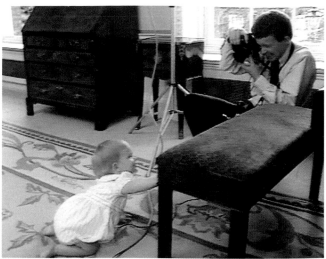

achieve. We've always hit it off very well and I just think she's marvellous.

'The story arose obviously because she wasn't chosen as a godmother for Harry. Had our child been a girl, the possibility was there, but Harry arrived so we went to a man.

'I've come in and the press have liked, perhaps, my clothes or my hair. I don't know: whatever it is, I haven't done the hard work she has.

'She works ten times harder than me and deserves every bit of credit coming her way.'

Does she think that some of the papers, as is often the way of life, build up people, and then just as quickly knock them down?

'Well, they do, but there again it's their job, isn't it really? I came in on the scene and I, apparently, could do no wrong. But it's quite interesting to see the niggly things that go on now, that, apparently, perhaps I could be doing wrong.

'I'm not asking to be perfect, I'm far from it, but I'd just like the chance and opportunity to get involved in my various interests that I've chosen without people talking about me being a shopaholic or something.'

The Prince agrees: 'It is true that, you know, this question of building people up on to a pedestal, the moment that happens, along comes a separate brigade that like knocking you off your pedestal. It's human nature, I suppose.'

So, talking of pedestals, what does he think about the people who say that some of his newer interests are just a bit eccentric. What about alternative medicine for a start? He is disarming:

'Well, yes, I think I'm becoming more eccentric as I get older, probably. Clearly, something

like – I prefer to call it complementary medicine – can easily be considered by people who don't think it has any relevance at all as eccentric.

'I can understand that. I also feel there are certain aspects of complementary forms of medicine which can have a great deal of value and effect for certain ailments. All I am making a plea for is a slightly more open-minded approach to this sort of thing than just to shut it off and say it doesn't exist.

'For hundreds and hundreds of years, thousands of years, such forms of medical treatment have worked, there's no doubt about it. But the trouble is they don't work for everybody: you have to find the right thing for each person.'

Is the same thing true of his interest in spiritualism, mysticism?

'Well, yes, absolutely. I've been riveted by the way in which all this has developed, because I've seen articles shown to me saying that I play with Ouija boards. I don't even know what they are. I've never seen one.

'I spend my entire time, apparently, trying to get in touch with Lord Mountbatten, and all sorts of other things. The answer is I don't, nor would I necessarily want to.

'I might as well say it, I might as well emphasise it, because I'm fed up with getting letters from people all the time saying "Don't touch the Ouija boards".'

The Prince believes the reports about him on this began as a result of his admiration for the late Arthur Koestler, the author who was greatly interested in parapsychology and left a bequest for a professional chair for its study in a British university – as it is already studied in the United States, the Soviet Union and continental Europe.

Told that no British university might take up the offer, the Prince, as Chancellor of the University of Wales, wrote to the Vice-Chancellor saying it would be a great pity to lose the bequest. The University Council did apply, but Wales, in the end, lost to Edinburgh. The Prince thinks that the publicity began with just that scientific proposal.

'What I find so annoying is that it should be reduced to this level of absurdity.

'I'm not interested in the occult, or dabbling in black magic or any of these kinds of things or, for that matter, strange forms of mysticism. I'm purely interested in being open-minded.

'After all, there are so many inventions, and things, which

Prince Charles visited India and Nepal in November 1980. During the tour he undertook a three-day trek in the Himalayas (left) and also visited the Golden Temple at Amritsar (right)

have been proved scientifically in the past, which everybody totally pooh-poohed before they were proven, and I think it is an area which is worth studying, sensibly and within the right scientific bounds.'

But is the Prince himself open-minded when it comes to modern architecture? Would some of the architects he's criticised – the extension of the National Gallery that he called a 'carbuncle' – think so? Is it part of his job to start controversy?

'I think so, yes, as long as it's not party political controversy. I open myself, don't I, to every kind of accusation? I'm only too aware of that, and I don't do it lightly. I take a deep breath, a very deep breath, because I know what's going to happen.

'I just feel sometimes, not too often, I can throw a rock into a pond and watch the ripples create a certain amount of discussion, hopefully to see whether something better can come out of it ultimately.

'With the architecture side of things I discovered through a little market research that a lot of other people who weren't architects shared my anxiety about the way in which things were going.

'So I plucked up my courage and I sat down and I wrote this speech and I asked people for help as well.'

That plan for the National Gallery was scrapped. Public opinion was with him. There may not even be hard feelings. The Prince is adept at seeing the other side to issues:

'I've met the architects of the National Gallery extension, and I've had them to dinner here, and we've had some very enjoyable discussions. It was almost impossible to produce something reasonable out of a brief like that which required a gallery extension and offices as well. I mean, it was almost impossible.'

And one more question – really a family one. Is the Prince now a vegetarian? He says:

'No, I'm not. I'm not a complete vegetarian, but I started to examine the things I ate slightly more carefully than I had done before. I actually now don't eat as much meat as I used to, I eat more fish.

'I actually find I feel better if I don't eat as much meat. After all, in our reasonably comfortable Western society we do eat a lot more meat than ever used to be the case and I think it can be overdone. After all, one is perfectly at liberty to have different outlooks on things one eats during different phases of one's life. It may be that in another ten years' time I'll go back to eating meat every day.'

Is the Princess thinking of following in his footsteps? 'I prefer fish to meat. But I don't think I'm going dotty.'

Do the children just like what they get? The Princess is succinct: 'They eat what they like. Anyway, it's cheaper to eat fish.'

But people have been worried. Does she eat enough? Often, it seems, there's just not enough time:

'When we go on an engagement, if it's a lunchtime one, we often have a buffet lunch so we can get around the enormous number of people there some-

times are. It's impossible to talk and eat at the same time, so you end up chasing a bit of chicken around the plate and then never getting anything yourself.

'And by the time you get home, certainly there's no time. You're rushing off somewhere else.'

So she doesn't diet? 'I'm never on what's called a diet. Maybe I'm so scrawny because I take so much exercise.'

She's always been interested in dancing – and she still keeps it up:

'I actually wanted to be a dancer, but I overshot the height by a long way. I couldn't imagine some man trying to lift me up above his arms.

'But I do it once a week if I can, and it's a combination of tap, jazz and ballet, and I really enjoy it enormously. I think it's vital to switch off for one or two hours every week. It's my absolute passion.'

Another passion is music, and she is proud of her post as President of the Royal Academy of Music. Her tastes are catholic, and her stereo headset is a constant companion, usually for classical music because she can get the pop she likes from the radio:

'I'm a great believer in having music wherever I go, whether it's a headset or a radio or a record player. And it's just a big treat to go out for a walk with music still coming out with me.

'I tend to listen to an enormous amount of classical music,

'Often there isn't time to eat lunch during an engagement' – although the royal couple enjoyed a hearty barbecue at the Speaker's residence, Kingsmere Farm in Ottawa, during their tour of Canada in 1983

The Prince has never worried greatly about his clothes. Since his marriage, however, the public no longer thinks of him as a prince in uniform. The Princess admits she may have influenced him a little – 'like maybe the odd tie' while the Prince says it is his choice of shoes she has helped him with. They are seen here in Milan in April 1985

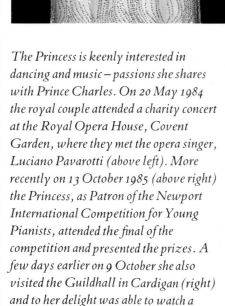

The Princess is keenly interested in dancing and music – passions she shares with Prince Charles. On 20 May 1984 the royal couple attended a charity concert at the Royal Opera House, Covent Garden, where they met the opera singer, Luciano Pavarotti (above left). More recently on 13 October 1985 (above right) the Princess, as Patron of the Newport International Competition for Young Pianists, attended the final of the competition and presented the prizes. A few days earlier on 9 October she also visited the Guildhall in Cardigan (right) and to her delight was able to watch a ballet class – 'I actually wanted to be a dancer but overshot the height'

whether it's Grieg, Rachmaninov or Schumann. All my family, my side of the family, are very music-oriented, and that's where I've picked it up. I love it.'

Has she set about changing Prince Charles's tastes? Certainly, they both enjoyed their time at the Bob Geldof concert. He says: 'It has been the greatest fun meeting a lot of groups and hearing their music which, I must admit, I hadn't heard much before – mainly because of the time factor, and I do like classical music. I like some pop music, not all of it by any means.'

She says, tactfully: 'I've got a reputation for liking all the people whose concerts we go to, and we go to raise money, hopefully, for my husband's charities. But both of us love classical music and the opera and the ballet, and go whenever we can.'

Anything else she might have changed? The Prince has never worried greatly about his clothes, unlike some of his predecessors. He has even borne with equanimity such criticisms as that of the Menswear Association that his clothes are 'dull and boring'. Has she tried? She says:

'Obviously one or two things, like maybe the odd tie or something . . .'

The Prince: 'Shoes.'

'Shoes. We won't go any further, but nothing dramatic.'

Do they really share an interest in polo, which she's been said to have called 'a nothing sport'? She's firm about that:

'I enjoy polo enormously. I mean, I go to as many matches

The Princess insists she likes polo and she goes to as many matches as she can. It is at polo matches that Tim Graham is able to capture some of their more intimate moments when they openly show their love and affection for one another – here at Cirencester on 30 June 1985

Among the penalties of the job the Prince and Princess of Wales face is the separation from their children when they go abroad. At the end of the tour of Italy in April 1985 both Prince William and Prince Henry flew out to Venice to be reunited with their parents (below) at the start of a private cruise on board the Royal Yacht Britannia

I can. So the myth about me hating it has really got out of control.

'I enjoy fishing too and we both do it.'

She is, in fact, a very good shot.

And do they occasionally have words when they're on their annual ski-ing holiday?

The Princess: 'That's the media saying it. We're OK, thank you, we're fine.'

The Prince: 'It may be that last year there was a misunderstanding about the actual plan for the press. Someone unfortunately altered what we'd been told, and she went one way and I went the other.'

So will they be going back again next winter?

The Princess: 'Yes, you might read another story next January. Mustn't disappoint you.'

These are among the penalties of the job, of the way of life, of being ambassadors, as the Prince says, which they have had to put up with. So is the parting with the children when they go abroad, and even when they are in this country, so that going home is, the Princess says, the best part of the day: 'Of course it is. Very much so.'

Had she realised quite what she was taking on: that she could never walk down the street again without all eyes being on her? 'No, I didn't.'

That she just cannot behave now as she used to? She laughs: 'I think that's probably just as well – if you knew how I used to behave.'

At which point there is a loud thump from overhead. It means Prince William is up from his midday rest.

WESTWARD, LOOK

The Prince of Wales has always been forgiving towards his great-great-great-great-great-grandfather, George III, who contrived to lose the American colonies. 'The tragedy is,' he said, after studying the archives at Windsor, 'that the American colonies never received a visit from him: if a royal tour had been a conceivable undertaking in the eighteenth century, the leaders of the colonies might have understood him better.'

The Princess hadn't been to America. She said: 'I go with an open mind. Much the easiest.' She does have long-lost cousins there. Among them, in the past generation, Ramon Novarro the silent cinema's heart-throb, and Humphrey Bogart. It's all part of the British connection.

They both see themselves abroad, and especially in America, as ambassadors for Britain, building good will – precisely where George III failed, though, the Prince thinks, he has had a bad press for a couple of centuries:

'It seems to me, in life, if you can actually meet the person concerned, very often a lot of the rumours and the strange stories about people can be dispelled when you actually come into contact with the individual.

'I just happen to have a certain degree of admiration for my forbear, King George III, because I think that he had a raw deal. So often history is composed by people who, inevitably,

53

During their interview at Kensington Palace the Prince and Princess of Wales explained that they see themselves abroad 'as ambassadors for Britain, building good will'. This they certainly achieved in Newfoundland in 1983 where the Prince opened the 400th anniversary celebrations in St John's; indeed, they hoped to foster more goodwill in the United States too (previous spread)

through no fault of their own necessarily, are biased one way or the other. I think George III suffered from a certain degree of bias politically.

'I think he was an enjoyable person to meet and was greatly loved in the latter part of his life – a bit priggish apparently when he was young, but aren't we all at some stage probably – and if he'd gone to the States I couldn't help feeling that they might have actually discovered what he was really like rather than being told something different.'

What would certainly surprise George III is that, one way or another, his successors have come closer than he ever did to recapturing the thirteen colonies. Two world wars have encouraged that. So, persistently, have the international media, radio and television, for more than half a century now. It is quite an achievement. The British political influence on United States policy has diminished pretty steadily in the post-war years. But American curiosity is undiminished, and even growing, in a royal family that much of the United States has come to adopt as its own.

There is nowhere in the world today, two centuries on, where the royal family is more effectively and regularly on display than the United States; and nowhere, more often than not, where its members, young and old, are surer to get an affectionate reception. In taking the Princess to Washington, the only surprise was that it had taken the Prince so long. The love affair between the United States and

British royalty has been common knowledge for most of this century; now, as hardly a month passes without a royal visit of one kind or another, it may even be time to appoint a royal resident in either Washington or Hollywood just to cope with the routine duties.

There have been royal visits of the first importance. That by the Prince's grandfather and grandmother, invited by President and Mrs Roosevelt in June 1939, the first visit by a reigning British monarch, was a conscious, deliberate effort on the very eve of World War II to show the world that the two democracies were, or were going to be, on the same side. Equally, what the Queen said in Independence Hall, Philadelphia, in July 1976, just 200 years on from the Declaration of Independence itself, was a unique admission in the relationship between any two states: 'Without that great act in the cause of liberty ... we could never have transformed an empire into a Commonwealth.' Out of respect for her ministers (and perhaps for George III) the Queen does not pass that kind of judgment at home.

Other comings and goings, of course, are merely trivial. That by the last Prince of Wales (Edward VIII) in 1924, when he got to know New York and bathtub gin, merely added to his father's blood pressure. Prince Andrew's antics with a fire extinguisher when he was trying to raise money for the British Olympics team in Los Angeles were even more juvenile, though the loyal British community, at least, still won't hear a word against him. But most serve a real purpose and are seen to do so. Whether it is the Queen herself getting drenched on the way to the Reagans' ranch above Santa Barbara, or Princess Alexandra helping out at an industrial fair in Minneapolis, or Princess Anne charming half of North Carolina on the 400th anniversary of the lost settlement at Roanoke, or the Prince's own next date in Texas, the relationship is a close one, and getting closer all the time. There are many parts of the Commonwealth that do not get such royal attention.

The Americans were very anxious to see the Princess, and to inspect her on their own turf, through their own eyes and, even more, the eyes of their own television and newspaper reporters. Their approval was evident and reassuring, but it was not lightly given. The British media, intensely protective of their own best, long-running family story, resent any criticism of the royal family which they do not originate themselves; so Canadians and Italians are not spared if they choose to point out, as they have, that the Queen is middle-aged or the Princess occasionally wears a dress she's worn before. But it is the American test that matters, if only because American curiosity is greater than any other; and American outspokenness, too.

Yet, as the Prince and Princess found, they had a lot going for them. America enjoys youth and wishes it well. It likes adherence to the ideal of the family. It does not matter that it voted last time for the oldest President in its

history, and the first divorced one. It is the hope, the ideals that matter. The Prince and Princess could not exactly miss. But there was more than that. Simply because the United States was created by the rejection of the British crown has never meant

George III (1760-1820) failed in forming good relations with North America and lost the American colonies – although Prince Charles suspects he got a 'raw deal'. Painted at Windsor (1799-1800) by William Beechey

that Americans do not or did not understand the crown. It was the British Parliament that disappointed Jefferson and Franklin, though King George the tyrant got the blame in American schoolrooms for a century and a half. Nor have Americans ever failed to follow what the crown was up to. When the young Victoria succeeded in 1838, the *New York Mirror* immediately noticed that 'we have Victoria bonnets, Victoria shawls, Victoria songs, Victoria marches, Victoria mint-juleps, and somebody has just opened a shop in Broadway which he calls "The Victoria Hair-Dressing Establishment".' Times do not change.

When Victoria and Albert rescued the monarchy from the reputation her uncles had given it, the point was far from lost in America. President Buchanan, writing to Victoria in June 1860 to suggest a visit by the then Prince of Wales (Edward VII), explained it would allow the American people to 'manifest their deep sense of your domestic virtues as well as their conviction of your merits as a wise, patriotic and constitutional sovereign'. It was not at all a universal view of monarchy. As late as Roosevelt's Lend-Lease Bill in 1941, an isolationist Congressman declared it would mean Roosevelt living in England and the King and Queen residing at George Washington's home at Mount Vernon. Prominent among the reasons why the isolationist distaste for the British crown has died away has been precisely the series of royal visits from 1860 onwards to 1985, and especially since the war. Famili-

arity, for once, has encouraged respect.

The United States has been in no danger of succumbing to monarchy in real life for over 200 years; so a substantial part of it, the romantic part, the sentimental part, the pro-British part, and, above all, the highly curious part (which may be predominantly feminine), finds it all the easier to do so in the imagination when monarchy is simply there on a visit, just passing through, or monarchy is there on the television screen on those increasingly numerous occasions when royal ceremony, as at royal weddings, attracts the attention of that majority of mankind that does not have a royal family.

In that way, especially to a country like the United States, accustomed to looking forward, not back, accustomed to seeing in Europe the very antithesis of its own history, a family synonymous with the world America once left behind and a family it can also like and enjoy and criticise and gossip about, almost as neighbours, will almost always be welcome. After all, most American Presidents are middle-aged, their children are few and forgettable, more than half the electorate has not voted for them, and their constitution forbids them to stay more than eight years in the White House. In this sense it is a continuing human interest, a human need, that the royal family fulfils in America. And it is a family that is noticeably ready to fulfil it.

As with all family relationships, there have been ups and downs. And as the relationship, of necessity, has been political, it has needed judicious nurturing. When President Buchanan wrote to Queen Victoria in 1860 he did so as a former Secretary of State and a former United States minister in London, so he had all the diplomatic credentials. He could also see that the Civil War (in which he was to support the Union) had become almost inevitable. Whatever he thought, he chose to invite the then Prince of Wales, a boy of nineteen, in the middle of the fierce election campaign that brought Lincoln to power and the South to secession – and Victoria agreed to it. Presidential and royal advisers ever since would not have countenanced any such thing, or would have been fired if they had.

In fact, the Prince of Wales had most trouble with the Orangemen of Canada, incensed at what they thought was his unnecessary politeness to the Roman Catholic bishops in Quebec. Twice, on his progress up the St Lawrence by steamer, he refused to land in order to avoid their demonstrations, and was hissed and groaned at by them in return. But in the United States there was hardly anything but enthusiasm. It was less than fifty years since Britain and the United States had been at war in the Great Lakes: the Prince had actually spoken to Canadian survivors of the campaign in which they had recaptured Detroit for the empire. But in the city itself 25,000 people packed the landing stage just to get a glimpse of Lord Renfrew (as he chose to call himself) and good-naturedly managed to push three of his officials into the river.

The American tour was the making of the Prince. Cooped up with his school books, knowing nothing of boys of his own age, not even allowed to live in college at Oxford, he found he liked America, Americans, American ways, American hotels; and he found Americans liked him. There was one culture shock, which later royalty had to learn to get over too: the American press. Used to the deference of the Court Circular, he was surprised to find, even in Canada, that details of how he had danced twenty-three times at a ball, the dresses and behaviour of the young women he danced with, and the time he tripped, were all telegraphed at length to the New York papers. It was said he had 'wept copiously' at one of the Orange demonstrations. But, even faced with his first experience of such imaginative reporting, he remained 'affable'.

He found the Chicago crowds friendly but 'quiet and orderly'. He went shooting on the prairie. St Louis, where 60,000 turned up at the cattle show, thought him 'unassuming'; so he was popular. Then, twelve hours a day in his railway carriage, he slowly went east: Cincinnati, Pittsburgh, Harrisburg, Baltimore, to Washington. He stayed at the White House, had dinner with the President and the Cabinet, watched a firework display in his honour, lunched at the Capitol, and planted a chestnut sapling near Washington's grave. Nothing was too good for George III's great-grandson.

In Philadelphia he went to the opera and found the crowd rising spontaneously to sing 'God Save the Queen'. Back in London *The Times* rebuked those who thought they saw a portent: 'There is not a sane man in the British Isles who would wish to see the United States once more ours, and governed by Queen Victoria, Lord Palmerston and the British Parliament. We have enough and too much already, with India added to our fifty dependencies...'

Others agreed. In Richmond, Virginia, soon to be the small capital of the Confederacy, the mayor and the Prince were inspecting a statue of Washington, when the crowd shouted at him: 'He socked it to you at the Revolution. Guess he whipped you Britishers.' The slave dealers, small planters and horse traders were getting truculent. In New York, too, the Irish members of the City Militia refused to parade for him, saying he was 'the representative of a government which has driven themselves from their homes, and which continues to destroy their kith and kin in the land of their nativity'. It still has a familiar ring.

It did not matter. The Prince's reception at the Battery was a triumph. The mayor forgot Lord Renfrew and addressed him as 'Your Royal Highness'. He drove up Broadway in an open barouche, built specially by the city at a cost of $1,000, to unceasing cheering. Half a million spectators lined the three miles of the route, controlled by only fifty policemen. Church bells tolled 'God Save the Queen'. The crush was so great at the Academy of Music ball that the centre of the floor gave way and fell three feet. Organisers of royal jaunts have been cautious about that ever since.

He went to Boston and Bunker's Hill and Harvard. He met Emerson, Oliver Wendell Holmes and Longfellow. When he got home his mother found he had got 'extremely talkative'. What it all demonstrated in fact was that the two English-speaking peoples, faced with new problems and uncertainties of their own, were capable of making up in public. They had moved on from the eighteenth century. Very possibly, they would not think of fighting each other again.

It was, of course, a royal intervention that helped to stop a war a year later. In America the War Between the States had begun. British sympathies were divided. As liberal opinion and the Royal Navy had been preeminent in ending the slave trade from West Africa, Lincoln's outright opposition to slavery itself won British sympathies. But the South had many admirers, and Lancashire's cotton manufacture depended on its trade; even more, in the early months, the conventional wisdom in London was that the South would win. So the British authorities were incensed when, on 8 November 1861, the Northern gunboat *San Jacinto* stopped the British mail packet, *Trent,* on the high seas and took off two Confederate ministers and their secretaries on their way to London and Paris.

War seemed likely. Lord John Russell prepared instructions to the British ambassador in Washington to get Lincoln to climb down or leave with all the members of the legation. Russell's despatch duly went out to Windsor for Victoria's approval. Prince Albert, already ill with typhoid (which his doctors denied), did not like it, and early on Sunday morning, 1 December, toned it down, suggesting that the captain of the *San Jacinto* might not have acted under instructions and asking only for the restoration of the four diplomats 'with suitable apology'. The Queen dutifully copied it out, and it was returned to the Foreign Office.

It helped to save the day. The American Secretary of State, William H. Seward, admitted he was relieved to find the despatch courteous and friendly. The four Southerners were freed by the North. And the Prince Consort, memorably, died. Annotating the paper, his widow emphasised: 'This draft was the last the beloved Prince ever wrote.' It was not, of course, the only factor. But if Britain and the United States had then let themselves get into the habit of going to war in the nineteenth century, the consequences in the twentieth would have been painful for both.

It was not in Victoria's nature, in her widowhood, to travel frequently beyond Deeside or the Isle of Wight. Edward VII, despite his American triumph, had come to prefer Biarritz or Paris (the state visit for which he is remembered) or the homes of his German cousins to far afield. His son, George V, having concluded that he had seen the world as a naval officer, preferred Sandring-

ham to anywhere, doubted the usefulness of royal visits at any time, and, after the Great War, stubbornly refused to travel beyond his former allies, France, Italy and Belgium. He was fond of saying the nearest he got to the United States was walking halfway across Niagara and taking off his hat. The place he liked was India, where his durbar in 1911 left an overwhelming impression on him and a determination to look after the interests of the Indians loyal to the crown. It was not that he disliked individual Americans. He had time for the Astors and the Vanderbilts, for Teddy Roosevelt, and for his nephew, the young Assistant Secretary to the Navy, Franklin. He entertained Woodrow Wilson whom he thought 'odious' on the President's Christmas visit in 1918 before the Versailles conference. He asked Charles Lindburgh, after his trans-Atlantic flight: 'One thing. How did you *manage*?' American ways were not his, and the more his eldest son admired them the more he distrusted them.

The Prince of Wales's visit to the United States in November 1919 was as big a public relations hit as his grandfather's had been. He had travelled energetically through Canada, and had even bought a ranch south of Calgary (which prompted George V to ask if he meant to buy a sheep station in Australia and an ostrich farm in South Africa) but nothing prepared him for the reception in the States. When he crossed the border at Rouse's Point station he was met by the Secretary of State, Robert Lansing, shook hands

people.' Roosevelt himself, who had been inclined to think of them merely as 'two nice young people', quickly recognised their calibre, finding the King a man with whom he could discuss serious things. He invited them to visit him and his family at his home at Hyde Park, in Duchess County, New York, and sat down in his library with his mother and family to welcome them.

The King and Queen had been at the World's Fair, in Flushing Meadows, where the crowds had sung 'Rule Britannia!' and 'Land of Hope and Glory', and on the ninety-mile journey up-state they passed through waiting crowds in the small towns, with car horns hooting, flowers strewn in the way, and church bells ringing. They were two hours late. As the car drove up at Hyde Park, a tray of cocktails was immediately presented. Roosevelt said: 'My mother thinks you should have a cup of tea. She doesn't approve of cocktails.' 'Neither does my mother,' the King said, and took one.

The President and King talked of the future until 1.30 am. In particular, Roosevelt expounded his idea of a chain of American bases to be established on British islands from Newfoundland south to Trinidad. That was to happen in 1940. King George, as King of Canada, had been accompanied by the Canadian prime minister, Mackenzie King. He said to him afterwards he wished his ministers in London would talk to him as Roosevelt had done. 'I feel exactly as though a father were giving me his most

careful and wise advice.' Roosevelt, in fact, had been too optimistic in what he believed he could manage with American opinion. The King even thought he had promised that if London were bombed the United States would go to war. But he had begun the generation of trust that was to matter so much within three months.

It was an important moment in the making of the decisive alliance of the war. It was also a visit that helped to make the King. It gave him greater assurance, and a growing confidence in his own judgment that was to stand him in good stead. He saw that a function of the new monarchy had to be to see things for himself, and to be able to

Princess Elizabeth and the Duke of Edinburgh visited the United States at the end of October 1951. The Princess was met by President Truman at Washington Airport

assess politicians around the world for himself. And he, in turn, showed North America what the model of a new monarchy was. Eleanor Roosevelt, visiting the King and Queen in Buckingham Palace in the war, found them shivering in the draughty rooms and hot water restricted by a line painted on the baths. In some ways theirs was a much more spartan life than their democratic politicians led.

This was remembered on a hazy evening, 31 October 1951, when the government offices in Washington closed early to let the workers see Princess Elizabeth of Canada and her husband drive through the streets to Blair House, where President Truman was living at the time. The President had been at the airport to meet them, recalling his meeting with her father off Plymouth after the Potsdam conference in 1945. After they had spent two days seeing the sights and receiving the Commonwealth ambassadors at the Canadian embassy, he told his royal visitors: 'It would be almost as hard to imagine a war between our countries as it would to imagine another war between the states of this country. It just wouldn't happen.'

Three years later, Queen Elizabeth the Queen Mother was back in the United States for the first time since she was there with the King, being shown round New York and speaking out at an English-Speaking Union dinner in a way she might not have chosen to do in London. She thought American policy-making happened 'in an atmosphere of considerable clatter', so 'we do

not always wait as confidently as we should for the final results, which are apt to be moderate, generous and wise'. She added: 'Similarly, people in the United States are inclined to misinterpret British policy, because we go about it in our own, quite different way.' She went on to Washington, to call on the Eisenhowers, and to Richmond and Williamsburg, visits remembered with affection many years later. It all underlined that the monarchy had long ceased to be a barrier to friendship in American minds; it had become the biggest public catalyst in the relationship.

American curiosity was at its height when Prince Charles and Princess Anne visited the Nixons at the White House in July 1970.

Royal visits to America have been many since World War II. The Queen Mother made a return visit in October 1954. The royal sightseer saw New York from the Observation Tower of the Empire State Building

didn't linger long outside the door for the press. Behind her she left local society counting its triumphs and bruises in the competition for places at the dinners and receptions. Did she worry about things like that? 'No,' *Newsweek* concluded, 'the Queen will go her own imperturbable way, and it is precisely because she rises above our petty jockeying for status that we cherish her.' Social observers even noticed that American women could now curtsey to the monarch without raising a single republican eyebrow.

The Prince of Wales knows the United States, although not as well as many Commonwealth countries. He has had shore leave in California; he saw eleven cities in October 1977, a work rate that won the compliment: 'You'd think he was running for office.' He was once even taken to hospital at Palm Beach, Florida, suffering from heat exhaustion: the nurse was careful to ask if he could afford to pay. In turn, much of the United States believes it knows him, and the Princess, from the day of their engagement on, from television. It has been from television, above all, and earlier from radio that America has developed its modern taste for the monarchy and all its doings.

It was, in fact, the abdication of Edward VIII in December 1936 that really dramatised the royal family for the American public – and it was radio that did it. His address to Britain and the Empire was picked up on the night by 300 American stations, reaching what was said to be an 'unprecedented audience'. Much more commentary on it from London was addressed to American listeners than the BBC of Reith allowed British ones. In addition, 160,000 words went by cable to the United States, a record since the armistice in 1918. The *New York Times* itself devoted nine pages to reports on abdication day.

The coronation of George VI and Queen Elizabeth the following May was carried in a radio broadcast beginning at 4.45 am on the east coast and lasting 6 hours 59 minutes on 300 stations, said then to be the longest continuous programme in American radio history. What irked the newsreels was that their first 7,000 feet of film was promptly viewed by the Archbishop of Canterbury and the Duke of Norfolk: they censored the shot of Queen Mary wiping a tear from her eye. Queens, it appeared, were not supposed to weep in public in cinemas.

After the war, the wedding of Princess Elizabeth and the Duke of Edinburgh got a two-hour early morning broadcast on the three networks. They pooled their coverage. But television was something different. It meant spectacle. It also meant rivalry. When the Queen was crowned in June 1953, the American networks vied with each other to be the first to put film from London on the air. (The race was actually won by the loyalists of CBC, who had enlisted the help of the RAF and the RCAF.) The *New York Times*'s television correspondent wrote: 'For all practical purposes today marked the birth of international television.' CBS declared: 'The day was a triumph for the whole television industry.' Television in the United States had now taken over from the radio and the cinema newsreels: since the coverage of Eisenhower's inauguration fewer than six months before the coronation, it had passed the point at which it was seen in over half of American homes.

So that when the Prince and Princess of Wales were married at St Paul's on that July day in 1981, the three American networks gave wall-to-wall coverage from dawn onwards. Many of their best anchor people turned up in London. They vied with the BBC and ITV for the best camera positions along the route. Their people had big briefing books about even the most recondite aspects of monarchy. And they voted it, as their viewers did, a spectacular success. It was international television at its best and happiest. Its star was the world's only international monarchy. That was precisely where George III went wrong.

On 29 July 1981 all three main American networks gave continuous coverage of the Prince and Princess of Wales's wedding. It was a 'spectacular success'

AT HOME IN THE COMMONWEALTH

The Prince and Princess, and their children, will spend much of their lives travelling the world, especially the Commonwealth. Already, with Australia, Canada and New Zealand visited together, they have pleased their admirers, made new ones, and helped to blunt the incipient republicanism that raises its voice at every pretended slight. This part of the job is central to their responsibilities.

The Queen herself has made the Commonwealth, black and white, a personal priority of her reign. She has been attentive, friendly and informed in visiting the countries of the old Empire that have gained their independence in her father's reign and in hers. She has faced danger and

opposition, as in Ghana in 1961 and French-speaking Canada in 1964; both were worrying times, if not visibly for her (she would never allow that), then for her ministers.

Her unrivalled knowledge of Commonwealth politicians and their interests has helped her to encourage sensible policies, as at Lusaka in Zambia, in July 1979, when the resolution of the Rhodesian issue might have taken quite the wrong turning. A century from now, the Queen's chief place in history may well be thought to be her nurturing of a Commonwealth that is still both identifiable and useful in the world.

For the Prince and Princess now it is a matter of trying to

build up similar experience and sagacity, and of earning similar respect. The airplane made the Prince the most travelled heir to the throne long ago. The Princess had not been far afield before her marriage. Both of them say that Australia, in particular, has done a lot for them. For the Princess her flight there in 1983 was a journey into the unexpected:

'The first week was a shock. It was like a baptism of fire, but having got into the feeling of it, it got better. By the time I left Australia I felt I'd actually been able to achieve something.

'I was so amazed that I was capable of that, that New Zealand got easier, and it's sort of built up from there. But people tend to think that if you're going to Australia or New Zealand it's a holiday, but actually it's our busiest time, much busier than over here.'

The Prince admits that, in many ways, Australia made him when he went to school there:

'The Australians and New Zealanders are very forthright people. I could easily have sunk, if you know what I mean, and I was on my own, chucked into the deep end.

'And in the end the Australians were extremely friendly and kind. But I rather like the forthrightness because it means you can be fairly forthright back again. And, you know, that's quite fun.'

He certainly remembers his schooldays with loyal affection:

'When I was at school, you know, there was a certain amount of Pommy this and Pommy that. But inevitably people have to get used to you and when they discover that you've got a reasonable sense of humour and can laugh at yourself –'

The Princess: 'Which you have.'

'The Princess was herself and the crowds loved her.' In Sydney (opposite) she was openly amused by her husband's speech during the visit to the Opera House. In New Zealand Prince William had a photocall (above) and the young family showed they were quite at ease during the session in the gardens of Government House in Auckland

The job of the Prince and Princess of Wales and their children is to travel the world representing the monarchy – they have already made several foreign tours. Before leaving for Australia and New Zealand in March 1983 the royal couple commissioned Tim Graham to take some official photographs (previous spread). Prince William was the youngest member of the Royal Family ever to go on such a tour. It lasted six weeks and ended on a spectacular note in New Zealand at Waitangi where the Prince and Princess attended a Maori gathering and were taken across the water in a war canoe (previous spread)

'– Yes, sometimes. Then it's all right.'

Australia has something special for the royal family. Even Queen Victoria, whose idea of a lengthy sea voyage was a trip across the Channel, was prompted to write in 1859: 'I am sick of all this horrid business of politics and Europe in general, and think you will hear of me going with the children to live in Australia.'

She never went there, of course. Nor did her son, the Prince of Wales (later Edward VII), who fancied the idea of a visit in 1880 and was promptly told the Liberal government would not contribute one shilling to what it suspected would be a pleasure cruise. He in turn was reluctant to let his heir (later George V) go there in 1901: he thought George should go off and help to govern Ireland. But he was overruled, and the then Duke and Duchess of York not only opened the first Australian Parliament at Melbourne, they took up the entirely novel idea of visiting the local chambers of commerce wherever they went. It wasn't thought to be royal, exactly, but old England needed the business.

The next Prince of Wales (Edward VIII) was in Australia and New Zealand in 1920. New Zealanders he found quite like people at home, but in Australia he was slightly taken aback by what he called the 'mass impulse to prod some part of the Prince of Wales'. Security in those days could be rudimentary. He left 'half-killed by kindness, loyalty and a demanding programme'.

His brother the Duke of York (George VI) was glad to be ordered there with his young Duchess (now Queen Elizabeth the Queen Mother) in 1927, although it did mean they had to leave behind their one-year-old daughter (now

the Queen). The Duchess got tonsilitis in New Zealand; the Duke unlocked the doors of the new Parliament building in Canberra. They were not able to go there again together. His final illness meant it was Princess Elizabeth and the Duke of Edinburgh who flew from Heathrow in their place on 31 January 1952, when, the strain on his face, he waved them goodbye. Five days later he was dead.

The Queen's first visit as head of the Commonwealth was in 1954, on her coronation tour, and she has often been there since on official visits (the royal 'walkabout' was invented for Australia and the first experimental one was in New Zealand), for the Commonwealth conference, and to open the Melbourne Olympics. She enjoys being there, and they respect her for the work she devotes to the Commonwealth and to them.

Even so, the Labour government of Mr Bob Hawke has been steadily reducing Australia's ties with Britain by abolishing the old imperial honours system, ending appeals to the Privy Council from Australian courts, and ending the remaining power of veto over the appointment of state governors. The Australians, like the Canadians, have worried over their national anthem and their flag (they have not found an acceptable substitute for that yet).

But that has not dimmed the admiration for the Queen herself felt by most Australians, including young Australians. Opinion polls come and go, but the number saying they could manage without the Queen has been pretty static at under one-third. There has usually been a

There were so many new things to see in Australia (opposite) – the Princess rode in a stagecoach at Sovereign Hill, a gold-rush town in Victoria in south-east Australia, while earlier in the tour she had studied the terracotta colours of Ayres Rock at sunset. The rock, at 335 metres high, is the largest monolith in the world and is situated south of Lake Amadeus in the Northern Territory

'The crowds grew apace with the media's almost unqualified approval.' At Sydney Opera House (below) thousands crowded on to the forecourt to see the Prince and Princess of Wales

small majority for the monarchy even among those under thirty. But republicanism has always been strong among the Catholic emigrants from Ireland, left-wing socialists, and the new Australians, especially from Greece and Italy, who have had no experience of the crown or its meaning. Among them especially, the Prince and Princess have been, and will remain, very much on trial.

That the Princess did spectacularly well on her first visit in March–April 1983 was almost universally acknowledged. From the royal landing (with Prince William, from whom she refused to be separated) at Alice Springs in the centre of the continent, she

was the main attraction, and to the crowds that turned out to see her she could do little that was wrong. It was, in part, her initial uncertainty that won her sympathy. But as she found her feet and discovered, delightedly, that she had only to be herself to please children and parents alike, so the crowds grew apace with the media's almost unqualified approval.

The Prime Minister himself was on his best behaviour, content to tell the BBC only that he did not think 'we shall be talking about kings of Australia for ever more'. He realised that the Prince had no intention of getting mixed up in any way with Australian politics; that the process of

people were not. Since then Canada has had many royal visits, many of them important in its relationship with the crown, though none more so than that by George VI and Queen Elizabeth in May 1939, a visit that dispelled talk of secession from the Empire and isolationism and neutrality if war came.

In turning out for the crown, as in much else, Canada is two different countries. The Maritime provinces, founded by loyalists who moved north after the British defeat in the American War of Independence, are exuberantly royalist to this day.

In June 1983 the Princess was to enchant the people of Canada too. She looked as beautiful as ever in a red silk two-piece suit when the royal couple visited the Legislature Building in Edmonton, Alberta, and in a day dress made up in the style of 1878 when she accompanied Prince Charles, dressed in a frock coat, on a visit to Fort Edmonton

English-speaking Canada from Ontario westwards is still predominantly loyal, and shows it. But it has never been easy for the British royal family to break down the cynicism and calculated uninterest of French-speaking Quebec. That is something the Prince and Princess have still to try together.

On their first visit in June 1983 they wisely started with the Maritimes and Newfoundland, where enthusiasm knew precious few bounds. All ages were entranced by her, the occasional young woman still tried to kiss him, and even the French television news service in Quebec nearby ran lengthy coverage – without any protests. There was no doubt whatever about public interest there. And although Ottawa proved more standoffish (they got only a fraction of the crowd the Queen did on her last visit) that was put down to the heat, humidity and the ability to see it all on television.

The particular interest of young Canadians set the psychiatrists off trying to explain the difference between the acclamation of the Prince and Princess and the Beatlemania that had hit the country twenty years before. It was solemnly and very properly decided that the new generation respected traditional values of morality, stability and the family. However that might be, the royal visitors dressed up in frock coat and long gown as for Victorian Canada at a barbecue sing-song in Edmonton, Alberta, joining in the singing and foot-stamping. Back in 1951, Canada, and Britain, had admired the newspaper pictures of the young Princess Elizabeth of Canada at her first barn dance.

The Princess of Wales had her twenty-second birthday at Edmonton, where the crowd stood in the rain to sing 'Happy Birthday', and the Prince opened the World University Games. Canada, which has sometimes seemed to live slightly uncertain of its identity beside the United States, had shown more than mere curiosity about its royal visitors this time. It took the two of them for what they were, without great political overtones, as an asset, a continuing focus for the expression of shared experiences and a shared outlook. And, after all, that is what good ambassadors are for.

'All ages were entranced by her' – meeting the people of Charlottetown, the capital of Prince Edward Island in the southern part of the Gulf of St Lawrence

The Prince and Princess of Wales are certainly at home in the Commonwealth, whether it be in Australia, New Zealand, Canada or any of the other sovereign independent states, with its population today at well over 1,000 million. Here they are seen in Canada signing the Visitors' Book at Summerside on Prince Edward Island (right), and at St John's, the capital of Newfoundland, the Princess talks to the policemen who formed a guard of honour when the Prince opened the city's anniversary celebrations

WALES'S PRINCE AND PRINCESS

Wales is a loyal and royal country, as the home of the Tudors should be. But, until now, that has been without much encouragement from the Princes of Wales. Eight of the twenty-one never visited the place, either as Prince or as King. To those who did, it brought little luck. Henry VII, a good Welshman, sent his eldest son Arthur off to live at Ludlow; there Arthur took his young bride Catherine of Aragon; and there Arthur soon died at Easter 1502. Charles I, needing Welsh support at the outset of the Civil War, sent his son and heir Charles to Raglan Castle in September 1642, where he raised recruits, many of whom were to die at Edgehill a month later. In three centuries that was all Wales got.

It is very different now. The twenty-first Prince of Wales since 1301 is the first to have learned Welsh (tutored by a nationalist).

He is, of course, Colonel-in-Chief of the Royal Regiment of Wales, Colonel of the Welsh Guards, Chancellor of the University of Wales (and an Hon. DLitt of the university), Chairman of the Prince of Wales's Committee for Wales, and even patron of the Welsh Association of Male Voice Choirs. Short of turning out for the national rugby fifteen (which hasn't really needed his services) there is not much more he could have done to identify himself with his principality. He is modest now about his command of the language: 'I was at Aberystwyth for three months, and I like to think I can pronounce it reasonably well when reading it, but it is an extremely difficult language. It requires a lot of practice and, you know, if you're going to speak it you've got to try to get it right because otherwise people say what's the point of speaking it?'

Wales's Prince and Princess: HRH The Prince of Wales, an official portrait of the twenty-first Prince of Wales in his investiture robes, 1 July 1969; and the Princess dressed in the Welsh national colours of red and green on the first day of the royal couple's tour of Wales in October 1981 (previous spread)

Wales was the first place the couple visited together after their marriage. The Princess remembers, 'The people who stood outside for hours and hours . . . in the torrential rain . . . . They were so welcoming . . . I was terrified,' – at Carmarthen on 28 October 1981 (below and opposite)

The Princess remembers her first visit affectionately, their first public engagement after they were married. It poured with rain pretty well throughout. 'But the people who stood outside for hours and hours, five or six hours in torrential rain, that's what I remember. They were so welcoming, because I was terrified, the most frightening thing I've ever done because I was just married, but they made it much easier for me.'

So centuries of princely nonchalance and neglect are long over. They do, however, offer a moral: how patient the Welsh have been.

The title of Prince of Wales was certainly kept up with diligence. George III's first son, who was to become the Prince of W(h)ales and George IV, was given it by letters patent when he was only five days old. His christening had to wait for a month. But the Welsh had to go to London to see him. At the age of four he charmed a Welsh charitable body, the Society of Ancient Britons, who waited on him, with a pretty speech and a gift of £100. But he was an advanced forty-two before the exceptional happened. In September 1806, on a visit to Shropshire, he was prevailed upon to set foot for an hour over the border in his principality and even to plant a young oak beside the road; it was duly railed in and marked with a plaque. He quickly retreated to haunts that suited him better.

But he did have the grace to go back. George IV was the first king since James VI and I to remember that there were three other countries besides England in the United Kingdom. In 1821 he went to Dublin, and the next year to Edinburgh. In Anglesey, on the way to Holyhead for his crossing to Ireland, he was warmly applauded. It seemed to stick in his mind. Liking decorations of all kinds, he planned to institute a Welsh Order of St David, to rank with the Thistle and the Order of St Patrick. He even picked fifteen Welshmen on whom he meant to bestow it. But he died before he could do anything, and his less sentimental brother dropped the whole idea. It has not been revived.

The next Prince of Wales, Victoria's heir, Albert Edward, born in 1841, was also given his title quickly, nearly two months before he was baptised. He was to be Prince for fifty-nine years, the longest ever. But in his highly disciplined upbringing Wales and the Welsh did not feature at all prominently. Still, the Welsh do not give up lightly. When they learned that their Prince was going to marry Princess Alexandra of Denmark the idea was born at the Caernarfon eisteddfod of 1862 to compose a celebratory anthem. It was called 'On the Prince of the Land of Hills', but the English, as usual, took it over, changed the words to 'God Bless the Prince of Wales', and it was the hit of the wedding – and of all princely appearances since. In fact, Bertie and Alexandra recognised that they had a responsibility.

In 1868, on the way back from Ireland, they went to Caernarfon themselves and were cheered to the echo. He did the honours by inaugurating the new water works, and they then proceeded in state to the grand banqueting marquee where '530 of the elite of Wales sat down'. But the Prince's patience, or his appetite, soon had enough. In a hangdog little speech he said he was sorry he had been so long in going to Wales, and regretted that 'the proceedings this day have been rather more shortened than was first intended'. They had had their lot. After all, the Duke of Sutherland, at Trentham Hall, expected him for tea.

What he did do with style in Wales was, as King, carry out the first royal tour wholly by car. That was in 1907, and the motor car was still rare – and risky. Another innovation followed under his successor. The royal family had had no great plans for the Welsh connection, but in 1911 one was thrust upon them. The MP for Caernarfon Boroughs, David Lloyd-George, then an ambitious Chancellor of the Exchequer, was persuaded of the political advantage to be got from a new, and expressly Welsh, royal ceremony. And it would be in his own constituency. King George V and Queen Mary agreed (it would be helpful with the difficult Mr Lloyd-George anyway), and much effort went into constructing a spectacular ceremony for something which had previously been brief and behind closed doors. The young Prince Edward himself, just seventeen, had, naturally, not

been consulted. He said later he went through it 'half fainting with heat and nervousness', but what lingered in his memory was the 'preposterous rig' of white satin breeches and a mantle and surcoat of purple velvet edged with ermine, the whole topped off with a chaplet of gold which he shuddered to think his naval friends would see him in. It was with relief that he heard, a month later, that he had been posted as a midshipman to unceremonial duties in an old battleship in the Home Fleet.

Edward did not especially interest himself in Wales in his work or his leisure, until the very end of his brief reign. He did let his driver and car transport copies of the official newspaper, the *British Gazette*, down to Wales in the general strike of 1926, and he did visit there himself. He even knew the Rhondda and the poverty of its villages before, as the shadow of abdication fell upon him, he spent two days there to try to cheer up what were called the depressed areas. He was resigned to what was to happen to him, and he thought, indeed, that 'Wales was a truly prophetic place in which to wind up the many years of my public life'.

He certainly worried the Baldwin government. Even a king, he was to say later, could see that something was manifestly wrong, and he was heard to say that 'something must be done' to repair the ravages of the inertia that had gripped the region. It did not go down well with the government that was meant to be doing things, and he reflected, sadly, that economic issues had

On 1 July 1969 at the Investiture of the Prince of Wales, the Queen presented the Prince to the Welsh people at Queen Eleanor's Gate, Caernarfon Castle (opposite)

made it almost impossible for the monarch to be 'free to move unhindered among his subjects, and speak what is in his mind'. His ministers thought he found it easy to speak his mind, knowing that he would be leaving the country within days.

And that was nearly that: except that, in September 1939, when he returned to try to get a job in the war, one that was offered him was that of Deputy Regional Commissioner for Wales. He accepted it. The offer was then dropped.

Prince Charles heard of his future sitting with his school friends in his headmaster's study at Cheam in 1958. He was only nine. The Queen's recorded voice at the Commonwealth Games in Cardiff declared: 'I intend to create my son Charles Prince of Wales today. When he is grown up I will present him to you at Caernarfon.' The boys applauded, though he said afterwards he was 'acutely embarrassed'. But the presentation was easier said than done. Welsh nationalism, its

heartland in the Welsh-speaking farms and villages of the north but trying to establish itself in the industrial south as the alternative to the Labour Party, was not in a mood to compromise with any British institution. At its core was the language. At its periphery were student protesters, and a fringe of bomb-makers.

As the 1960s progressed, nationalism's political advance reached what was to be its apogee – although no one, least of all English politicians, knew it then. So the investiture planned for July 1969 began to look like precisely what the royal family's advisers did not want it to be: a trial of political strength in which the monarchy itself was being made the issue. Those who knew Welsh opinion were convinced that the investiture should go ahead, but no one could be sure about the ambitions and ingenuity of the bomb-makers. The Prince himself largely defused things by going to the university at Aberystwyth and succeeding, in a crash course, in

mastering Welsh sufficiently to make an effective eisteddfod speech, and, by his patience, persuading all but the hard-line students that he was a reasonable, accommodating young man who was only doing his job.

The police did find guns and gelignite, bombs did go off (one killed the two men planting it), but Welsh opinion grew increasingly royalist. The Duke of Edinburgh said afterwards: 'It was quite obvious that a very large proportion of Welsh opinion favoured having the investiture.' The nationalist party, Plaid Cymru, split openly over the issue. On the day in Caernarfon, it was the crowds who decided it, unequivocally. With one desperate moment, when he found he was sitting on his speech, the Prince, and the Queen, carried it off well: 'I, Charles, Prince of Wales, do become your liege man of life and limb and of earthly worship, faith and truth I will bear unto you to live and die against all manner of folks.'

It looked well in the castle. It looked well on television around the world. The Prince himself understood better than many of the politicians the sincerity of the nationalist feeling. But, even in the general election the following year, Plaid Cymru got only 11.5 per cent of the Welsh vote – and declined thereafter. It turned out that it was a United Kingdom after all.

Sensibly, after their marriage, the Prince and Princess made Wales the first place that they visited together. Much of the time they spent in driving rain. That did not put them, or the crowds, off. There were two fire bombs: one found at an army recruiting office, the other at British Steel's headquarters in Cardiff. There was a demonstration by students at Bangor; a paint spray was inaccurately directed at the royal car in Caernarfon. Though these matters

The Princess's recent visit to Wales was a far cry from her first visit four years ago. On 9 October 1985, an altogether more confident and relaxed Princess visited Royal Aircraft Establishment, Aberporth, near Cardigan in Dyfed, where she inspected Youth and Apprentice Training (opposite). On the same day the Princess also visited the Guildhall in Cardigan where she watched a first aid class (below)

were faithfully reported, at the end of the 400 miles they hardly seemed to matter. The Princess tactfully wore the Welsh colours of red and green on the first day. The crowds took her to their hearts as the wife of 'Carlo bach', and he adapted quickly to the demands, along the roads, to see her. 'I'm sorry,' he said, 'there's only one of us. I haven't got enough wives to go round...' and again: 'I'm just a collector of flowers these days. It's my role.'

What was plain, from industrial Shotton in the north to the Rhondda, where the welcome was warmer than anywhere, and Cardiff, where the Princess got the freedom of the city, was that the popularity of the two, and the trust put in them, far outweighed political considerations. Here was a Prince descended not only from the much disliked Edward I but from Llewelyn the Great, the last native Prince of Wales, and even from the great Owain Glyndwr, the last native Welshman to be proclaimed Prince. His sincerity was recognised; and she could do no wrong. They went back across the border with many presents, among them a Welsh black heifer called Sandra and a woolly black Welsh mountain sheep, but above all with the principality's evident affection. Wales had a Prince and Princess it wanted.

AMBASSADORS IN EUROPE

The Prince and Princess will be expected to be good Europeans. After all, within its common external tariff border the European Community is, in its way, the last of the great monarchical clubs. Half of its twelve members (as Luxembourg has its Crown Prince) are countries with crowned heads; and that is more than half the crowned heads still remaining in the world who need to be taken seriously. Among them all, it is the British royal family alone that is front-cover, front-page material everywhere. It is especially so in Europe.

This is not necessarily all to the good. Reading the European press does nothing for the royal blood pressure. The Queen, if she cared to read it at all, can never be surprised to learn that she is constantly on the point of abdicating, or that the Duke of Edinburgh is seriously ill, or that Princess Margaret has done, or is about to do, something or other extraordinary. The Prince of Wales, naturally, has been married off many times. The Princess of Wales is regularly about to be pregnant; the Italian papers were sure of it during the visit there in April–May 1985. Nothing is too improbable to bear wide repetition.

All this curiosity, this interest, is stirred up by the apparent invulnerability of the British monarchy's popularity. Although the British media, in their way, are often just as insulting by affecting to ignore the other European royal families totally

(unless there is real scandal) for the gossipy goings-on in and around Monaco, much of Europe is still fascinated by monarchy, and some of the Queen's fellow heads of state perform active and important constitutional functions.

The Queens of Denmark and the Netherlands are accustomed to helping to settle the formation of coalition governments. It is only among the more belatedly insular of British politicians that there is any surprise that, if there were a hung Parliament at Westminster after the next general election, the Queen would be the constitutional figure playing, with advice, just such a part. King Baudouin in Belgium regularly has a key role in keeping his governments going and his country together. In Spain, King Carlos himself is the last political defence against another resort to dictatorship.

So much of Europe expects to see active royal figures earning their keep. It expects, especially, to see good causes fostered by young people who are used to doing more than be decorative and enjoy themselves. There is still, plainly, a place for state visits, although the old belief that courts actually influenced alliances was disproved in Victoria's own day, and no one could have tried harder to run things than she did.

She invited the Orleanist King of France, Louis Philippe, to Windsor in 1844 and was thrilled

Ambassadors abroad again, the Prince and Princess of Wales visited Italy in 1985 on their first official tour of a country outside the Commonwealth. The tour was an undoubted success beginning in Sardinia on 19 April and ending in Venice on 5 May (previous spread) A warm welcome for Prince Charles in Milan (above) and an evening at La Scala (right) for a performance of Puccini's opera 'Turandot'. The Princess wore a stunning yet simple dress of silk chiffon – a practical style for formal occasions.

The Princess says of the trip, 'I was going along to support the British flag, with my husband as his wife. My clothes were far from my mind.' However, she couldn't fail to impress with the jaunty outfit she wore to the naval base at La Spezia (overleaf)

On 24 April the Prince and Princess visited the Cathedral in Florence and the church of Santa Croce during the morning followed by a tour of the Uffizi Gallery in the afternoon (above left). On the first day in Rome, 26 April, the royal couple attended a lunch at the Casina Valadier (above right)

Two days were spent in Florence – 'Through churches, galleries, palaces they went.' The Prince and Princess thrilled the crowds by trying out their Italian – seen (opposite) during a walkabout in the city.

that he was 'the first King of France who ever came to pay a visit to the Sovereign of this country'. But when he turned up in exile she invited the once-hated Bonapartist, Napoleon III, and the Empress Eugénie in April 1855, and was greatly taken by him. He knew exactly how to play her, and by that August she was in Paris, standing at Napoleon I's tomb. It all came to nothing. She married her daughter, the Princess Royal, to the liberal Crown Prince of Prussia but, even had the Emperor Frederick not died early, Bismarck would have settled policy. The 'grandmother of Europe' was only that – and hardly anything more.

George V, though, was wrong, for once, when he de-

clared abroad to be awful. It might have been for him, speaking no language but English, and he was reacting, anyway, to the exaggerated praise given to his father for his part in popularising the Entente Cordiale. But no royal family, least of all the British one, has been able to live in splendid isolation from the day of his death to this.

The visit of King George VI and Queen Elizabeth to Paris in July 1938 helped to keep the alliance together until Munich, if it did nothing more. Since the war the visits by President Mitterrand of France and, before him, President Giscard d'Estaing and President de Gaulle, could never remove the post-war edginess in Franco-British relations, but they helped to remind everyone that

Elsewhere in Europe the Princess of Wales visited West Berlin on 18-19 October 1985 as Colonel-in-Chief of the Royal Hampshire Regiment which is currently serving there. The Princess reviewed the troops of the 1st Battalion and met members of the regiment and their families. During her stay she donned a track suit for a driving lesson in a 15-ton tank in the parade ground (following pages)

BRINGING UP THE PRINCES

The most important single job that the Prince and Princess of Wales have now is bringing up their children.

But they haven't made up their minds about schools yet. The Princess says: 'I think it's too soon really. William's only three and Harry one. And I think there's no hurry at all until we see what sort of characters they're going to produce as they get older, and then find a school that they can adapt to. Certainly, if William likes outdoor life we'll find a school that has that as its main feature.'

The Prince is not the sort of father who automatically puts his sons down for his old school. In fact, they're not down for anywhere: 'I would hope that eventually there would be room somewhere. But it's always a difficult one, because whichever we do people will say we shouldn't do. Anyway, when it comes to my old schools I'd have to go and look at them again to see what they're like. There's been a lot of changes since my day and I may not agree with them, or we may not agree with the headmaster's outlook and so on. There's a lot of imponderables.'

Neither of them looks back on going away to school with pleasure. The Prince says: 'No, I didn't because home always was very happy and provided all the sort of things that I enjoyed. Some aspects of school were all right, but I found in those days that we hardly ever got out. We

only had three weekends a term; we never had any half-term. It was like, in a sense, prison.'

The Princess, too, has mixed memories: 'There were a lot of tears, because I hated leaving home. But I've built up so much from it . . . maybe not in the academic world. I love being outdoors, and I was captain of this and that, and I won endless cups for diving and swimming, which I adore. That's why I really enjoyed it, just having lots of friends.'

They will never be short of advice. The trouble is that royal families have seldom been very good at educating their offspring. Virtuous kings who have been the pillars of family life, like Charles I and George III, ended up with licentious sons who either ended (James VII and II) or nearly ended (George IV and his brothers) their dynasties. The much-married Henry VIII, though, produced two able intellectuals (Edward VI and Elizabeth) who determined the country's life and thought for over half a century. It is all very difficult, so difficult that many royal parents have simply reacted against their own experience and upbringing. It hasn't been a happy story.

The Princess says, 'We're open minded about William and his education . . . the bad luck about being number one is trial and error. Number two skates in quite nicely.' The Princess often spends time with her sons in the day room at Kensington Palace. She is seen here helping Prince William with his jigsaws. Not wishing to be left out Prince Henry joins in the fun before they both enjoy a ride on their rocking horses

George III was brought up almost entirely in an adult world. He was the first king to study science and he knew some French and German, but these accomplishments were less important than his loneliness and shyness, which made him a countryman; they also made him a remarkable collector of books, the originator of the King's Library at the British Museum. When it came to educating his sons he tried to make sure they worked, too, and soon spotted signs of dissipation in his heir, but he was lenient with their faults, told the Prince of Wales 'I wish more and more to have you as a friend', and gave him the liberty that was precisely his undoing.

Victoria had a gentle education and, as she was bright, responded to it: it was a means of mental escape from an overbearing mother. As heiress-presumptive, she was examined by the Bishops of London and Lincoln when she was not quite eleven, and deemed to be properly acquainted with all the required subjects from scripture through to Latin, geography and English history. She was taught French and German and could, while still young, converse in both, though she later denied that she spoke German with great fluency – and, writing her early love letters to Prince Albert, apologised for breaking into English because her German wasn't quite up to it.

Both Victoria and Albert had been scandalised by her uncles and were determined that their eldest son, Bertie, should not go the same way. They set their faces against sending the Prince of

Wales to school, where he would be bound to be infected by the frivolities of the aristocracy. The aim was to make the unfortunate boy 'the most perfect man', and he was expected to develop the intellectual equivalent of, at least, a Cabinet minister's mind. So, once governesses had made him trilingual as a child, he was turned over to relentless study, without encouragement and without friends; his father supervised it all personally, even reading his essays and exercises. The Prince duly developed tantrums and shouting fits.

Because Victoria survived so long, it is difficult now to believe that she lived in constant fear that she would die prematurely, probably in the childbirth that she so disliked, and so all the more pressure was put on Bertie to ensure that he would not ruin the monarchy by going to the bad. They let him go to Oxford but insisted that he should not live in college, where he would have to meet other young men. The result was that Bertie did go to the bad, in the army, with a young actress at the camp at the Curragh, in Ireland. It was the start of an enjoyably chequered career.

Naturally, after his upbringing, the Prince did not marry an intellectual. Lady Frederick Cavendish noticed: 'Neither he nor the darling Princess ever care to open a book.' Naturally, too, he insisted on a happy, protected family life for all his children. His mother was alarmed: 'They are such ill-bred, ill-trained children. I can't fancy them at all.' Still, the Queen was forced to admit that it might be better to send the boys

to school if only to stop them turning out like Bertie himself. She would not have Eton: it was much too near the temptations of London. The new, and distant, Wellington, she thought, would be preferable.

But the eldest boy, Prince Eddy, was backward and largely dependent on his brother Prince George, who was destined for the navy. So they were both sent to Britannia. The Queen was still unhappy. What she called 'a nautical education' would, she believed, be bound to bring on 'the prejudices and peculiarities' of British nationalism, which had turned out so badly with George III and William IV. The mother of monarchical Europe saw herself as nothing if not an internationalist.

They were bullied at Britannia. 'I'd get a hiding time and again,' George V recalled. They called him 'Sprat' because he was so small. But he liked the life. He found advanced mathematics no problem. He rose to command a torpedo boat and then a first-class gunboat. But Prince Eddy's eventual death left the next in line with little enough formal learning to fall back on. He needed languages, not seamanship, and he found German 'very difficult and it certainly is beastly dull'. His father, taking him to visit Bismarck, had to apologise for his son's deficiency. But it was more than that. Well into manhood George V could not spell Shakespeare correctly. Well into his reign he was still trying to complete his education.

Naturally, therefore, when it came to educating his sons, he

distrusted intellectuals and scholarships. When Prince Edward was trying to pick up an idea of party politics, George V refused to let him read any newspaper more contentious than *The Times*. Nor, he thought, did Eton have enough discipline. So Prince Edward and Prince Albert were sent off to Osborne and Dartmouth to train to be naval officers. After all, if their companions were going to be serving officers at sea, they would not be likely to make a nuisance of themselves, turning up in later years claiming to be close friends and wanting favours. So they went and were duly bullied in turn: Prince Edward was duly called 'Sardine' because he was so small. Dartmouth may have made them good naval officers. Prince Albert, though on the sick list, fought his guns in HMS *Collingwood* at Jutland. But though the King did pull his heir out of the navy and sent him to Oxford, where he lived in college, Prince Albert's achievement in passing out 61st of 67 in his year at Dartmouth was not the ideal training for a man who was to become King – and in 1936, when he did, he knew it only too well.

King George, after that experience, and Queen Elizabeth did not send their daughters away to school. There had been no precedent for that anyway, and the Queen herself was not anxious to push them into higher education, as she had not been

Prince Henry's very first steps made on 22 October 1985. Prince William gives a helping hand to his younger brother before he launches out on his own

pushed. She wanted them 'to spend as long as possible in the open air, to enjoy to the full the pleasures of the country, to be able to dance and draw and appreciate music, to acquire good manners and perfect deportment, and to cultivate all the distinctively feminine graces'. The war, too, meant that Princess Elizabeth and Princess Margaret had to learn their lessons behind the walls of Windsor Castle; it helped that the vice-provost of nearby Eton was at hand to instruct Princess Elizabeth on constitutional affairs. It happened partly by chance. What mattered was that the formula, however devised, worked.

Even so, Queen Elizabeth and the Duke of Edinburgh had very different ideas for their eldest son. Public opinion appeared to agree that he should mix with other children; Labour MPs believed that should be with children at a state school. That was expecting too much of everyone, not least the restraint of the media. So Prince Charles had to go off to a prep school, Cheam, in Hampshire, where he was a quiet boy, conscientious, good at English, but already aware that he was somehow on his own. He was to feel that even more when he moved on to his father's old school, Gordonstoun, in the north of Scotland, where he had to grit his teeth to get on in an establishment whose life was not

one he would have picked for himself. He was not helped by press excitement over a glass of cherry brandy he ordered in a Stornoway hotel and a stolen exercise book of his which turned up on offer for publication.

It taught him not to flinch, and that, too, was to help him when he went for seven months to Timbertop, the country camp of Geelong School, where he learned much about Australia – and about himself. His equerry said afterwards: 'I went out there with a boy, and returned with a man.' Back at Gordonstoun, he sensed he had succeeded: he became head boy (pleasing his father, who had done the same), and getting the A-levels which qualified him for

university in his own right, the first member of the royal family ever to achieve that. He could honestly say that he was glad he had gone to Gordonstoun which 'developed my willpower and self-control, helped me to discipline myself'. He went up to Cambridge, to Trinity, to read archaeology and anthropology and determined to get a degree, again the first member of his family to do so.

He might even have got a better degree than he did (a second) if the duty of being the Prince of Wales had not called him away for a summer term to study Welsh at Aberystwyth before his investiture in 1969. He managed it; Gordonstoun and

'He's surrounded by a tremendous amount of grown-ups, so his conversation's very forthright.' Indeed, Prince William was not at all shy at meeting the Commander of the Parachute Regiment and the Red Devils team when they parachuted into the gardens of Kensington Palace in May 1985. The display was also watched by Prince Charles, Colonel-in-Chief of the Paras

LEARNING ALL THE TIME

They and their children are already the world's most identifiable young family. That will be so well into the twenty-first century. It is as important to the country as it is to them that what they represent in people's eyes is seen to be relevant to the needs of the changing times. It is going to be quite a burden. Prince Charles does not talk about the future of the monarchy. He believes that is best done by the Queen alone. But what the Prince and Princess, and everyone else, can be sure of is that there will be surprises.

In the world into which he was born in 1948 few people, even with the example of India and Pakistan before them, supposed that the countries that were red on the map and owed direct allegiance to the crown would dwindle so rapidly. Even in 1961, the year of the Princess's birth, few supposed that unemployment in Britain would reach into millions again, or that rioting and burning would become almost endemic in some big cities, or that drug-taking would spread so rapidly and widely through much of a young generation.

It is no part of the royal responsibility to react immediately to each and every issue and national worry. The rights of the sovereign are still, as they were a century ago, the right to be consulted, the right to encourage, and the right to warn. But, in a real sense, the second and third of these apply nowadays to the

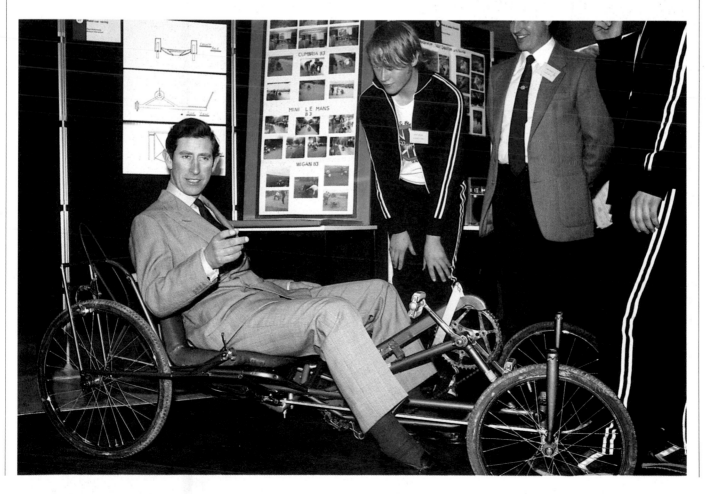

In October 1985 the Prince and Princess visited the Leith Enterprise Trust near Edinburgh. The Prince, Duke of Rothesay, is President of Scottish Business in the Community. During the visit the Prince was greeted by a guard of honour of the High Constabulary of Leith before meeting the people whose businesses have been aided by the Trust (above and opposite)

'It is more than anything else a way of life' – this is how the Prince of Wales sees his job. The royal couple are learning all the time whether meeting the people or concerning themselves with special causes. As Lord of the Isles the Prince took the Princess to meet the people of the Western Isles in July 1985. In December 1983, the Prince, concerning himself with people in the inner city areas, visited a Prince's Trust Project at a Community Centre in Manchester (previous spread)

sovereign's eldest son and his wife too. As part of the old mystery of monarchy is necessarily given up in a less deferential world, so the public interests of the royal family have become all the more significant.

It is evident now that some royal occasions that were taken for granted a decade ago are beginning to look strangely old-fashioned. It is very fine to launch a big ship or open a new canteen: it confers an enviable distinction on the workers there. But it may be becoming more widely appreciated that the royal duties that matter are now in more difficult causes.

So the Prince has been getting on with plans and schemes like his Youth Business Initiative, which has just given its thousandth grant of £1,000 to young

people needing a start in business. He says: 'I've been very much involved in this since those rather dreadful riots in Toxteth and elsewhere in 1981, the year we were getting married.

'I got together some of the people in my trusts and we worked out a scheme because I felt very strongly that we ought to try to enable young people in rather deprived parts of the country, in inner city areas and so on, to start their own enterprises, because I believe there is a great deal of talent which lies under-utilised.

'It's only a very small pinprick in terms of the overall problem. But, at least, I feel it's trying to do something.'

The man who got the thousandth grant had started a carpet and mattress cleaning firm,

arranging for it to be top of the list in the Yellow Pages, and now employing two other people part-time. His parents came from Antigua. What delighted the Prince, too, was meeting a group of Boston businessmen, who'd developed a similar scheme, based on his, for their own young people: 'This is one of those extraordinary occasions when, much to my amazement, the Americans have actually learnt something from us.'

For her part, the Princess, admiring Princess Anne's work for the Save the Children Fund and sharing the Duchess of Kent's concern for hospices, is widening her interests among the caring services. One of her chief interests is helping the deaf; though she is not quite as good at the sign language yet as she'd like to be: 'Well, I'm trying, but I think it's important to show that you're interested and you're not just breezing in and out, having seen them for a morning. I've got all my senses and they haven't, and I'm learning how they adapt, or if they've been deaf and dumb since birth how they cope, and how they deal with the outside world that doesn't always want to know about them.'

Both have had to learn the hard way about the risks in the world of terrorism and violence in which they have to move: the Prince with the murder of his great-uncle and friend, Lord Mountbatten, both with the assassination of President Sadat

The Princess, in widening her interests among the caring services, says on the subject of drugs, 'I felt I could start off by showing some interest, and not just going to an engagement and then walking away.' On 8 October 1985 she visited St Giles Hospital Drug Dependency Clinic in London (opposite left). Two days later she was in Salford greeting the crowds and talking to the families of mentally-handicapped children at Dr Barnardo's (opposite right and above)

of Egypt, who had entertained them at the end of their honeymoon. They were both 'shattered', the Prince says, at the death of Sadat who had been so kind to them: 'But, well, he was a Head of State, which we're not, and he was also a politician and living in the forefront of politics and controversy, which we're not. But obviously there is that awareness that something of that nature could happen, I suppose, to people in our position, and there are those who might want to do something unpleasant.

'I think you can only be fatalistic, otherwise you would probably go dotty.'

The Princess remembers: 'He was just such a special man when he came to see us, and it was so

sad because he was doing wonderful things in his country, and one minute he was there, the next minute he wasn't. And that's the awful thing: you can't ever see them again.'

They are properly reluctant to see themselves in any way the national exemplars of family life, and of a normally happy family life, although that is precisely what prompts much of the admiration and curiosity and, perhaps, envy. In the end the Prince admits it is a responsibility: 'I have a feeling it probably is. The essential thing is that it is a family operation, and that clearly is important, the way you live your family existence. The interest, for instance, that there is apparently in our two sons shows this.

Today the royal duties that matter are in more difficult causes and royal patronage can prove invaluable. On 2 October 1985 the Princess visited the London Headquarters of Help the Aged of which she is patron (top). The following week she visited St Anne's Hospice in Manchester (centre) and St Joseph's Hospice in Hackney, London (below). Her busy itinerary also included a visit to Newport on 13 October (opposite)

'I think people like to see people being happy if possible, and of course it puts a considerable pressure on anybody in that situation because we are only too aware of the hideous responsibility.'

So has the Princess's responsibility in this royal way of life turned out as she'd expected it would when she got engaged?

'I don't think anyone can tell you what's going to happen until you go through the experience yourself. My husband's taught me all I know.'

But did she find it difficult to adapt?

'I did, yes, purely because there was so much attention on me when I first arrived on the scene and I wanted to get my act together, so to speak, and I had so many people watching me the pressure was enormous. But as years go on it gets better.

'I'm still learning all the time.'